10 REASONS WHY THE RAPTURE MUST BE LEFT BEHIND

S. D. Morrison

Table of Contents:

Introduction: A Bit of My Story

The rapture haunted me as a boy.

I remember many years ago a particular night of sleepless, restless agony. I believed with all my heart that Jesus was returning that night, and I knew I didn't want to miss it. As I desperately stared out my window eagerly expecting the return of Christ, I prayed that God would not forget me or leave me behind. I had heard the stories, I knew what was coming next. It was way passed my bedtime, but I stayed awake long into the night, my little heart full of fearful expectation.

But nothing happened.

The rapture didn't come. I walked around school the next day saying to myself, "This isn't real. Today shouldn't exist. Last night was supposed to be the end of the world."

Like many young boys who grew up in a Christian environment, I was fascinated with the rapture. I was never a very disciplined bible reader, but when it came to the book of Revelation I was fiercely driven. I would read that book again and again and again desperate to find its hidden meaning. It was like a puzzle, an enigmatic collection of visions left for me to figure out.

I will never forget that night and the many other moments of terror I felt growing up in the shadow of the rapture. It wasn't until my college years that I began to study the scriptures more seriously. To my profound delight and shock I soon discovered how little there was to back up my belief in the rapture. And as I studied more, my faith in the rapture quickly faded.

My fears were relieved.

But not everyone has come to this conclusion. Many, especially today in America, still live under the belief that at any moment Jesus will come back and suck all the "true Christians" up into the sky and leave the rest of humanity on earth to suffer a great tribulation.

And that is why I've written this book. It was a little over a year ago now that I first shared my new-found understanding of the rapture in an article on my website. It quickly became one of the most read I've written. So I realized there was a need out there that I could fill. My story is not an isolated one. Many others share my experience. It's a big deal for me then to know that what I came to discover in my own life might also help someone else in theirs. And perhaps that's why you've picked up this book. Maybe you have questions about the rapture, maybe what once seemed so clear no longer seems that way anymore. I hope my story and the conclusions I've come to will help you leave the rapture behind for good.

I know firsthand what it's like to give up the pessimistic rapture and see God's hopeful end. To have hope for the future, to know that the world will be reborn and not destroyed. I know the joy I felt when I finally left the rapture behind. I hope to share that relief with everyone I can.

What you believe about the end matters. It matters because it changes how you live right now, and what sort of life you build for tomorrow.

I present here ten reasons why the rapture must be "left behind". I know not everyone will be convinced, and I'm sure in such a short book there will be many unanswered questions, but if just one person can find the courage to leave the rapture behind for good I will be exceedingly happy.

Though more of a primer of sorts, I hope this book will convince you to leave the rapture behind. May what I've written here launch you into a life of radical hope, one which sees good on the horizon and not dread.

So, without further ado, I present to you ten reasons why the rapture must be "left behind".

S. D. Morrison

Acknowledgments

I'd like to thank Kris Vallatton, though you may never read this, as I begin. Your lectures on eschatology remain some of my favorites to this day. Thank you for infusing hope and life into the future for me.

I also must mention two dear friends who were kind enough to look over the early drafts of this book. Tim Heath and Gordie Whitney thank you for your valuable input!

Ten Reasons Why the Rapture Must be 'Left Behind'

1. The rapture is scripturally unfounded.
2. The rapture is historically inconsistent with the teachings of the church for two millennium.
3. The rapture promotes escapism, a form of the gnostic heresy.
4. The rapture is driven by a fear based philosophy, and therefore inconsistent with a God of love.
5. The rapture teaches an baseless, pessimistic worldview.
6. The rapture implements a poor hermeneutical principle, often known as literalism.
7. The rapture is based on inconsistent hermeneutics, cherry picking when to use one method over another.
8. The rapture implies a second and third coming of Christ where the scriptures do not.
9. The rapture creates a Jesus inconsistent with the Jesus of revelation as witnessed to in the New Testament.
10. The rapture perverts Jesus' mission of bringing the Kingdom of heaven to earth into escaping earth for heaven.

1: Scripturally Unfounded

"The bible says it, I believe it, and that settles it."

What a strange saying! Whenever I hear it I think: "Well, that's a nice idea. But if it's really that simple, why can't Christians ever seem to agree on what it says?" If you can just pick up the bible and understand it without any prior knowledge, context, or study—that is, if the bible is such an *easy* book (as this phrase seems to imply!), then why are there over 30,000 Christian denominations worldwide? Why can't we agree on the bible if it's so easy to just read it, believe it, and have our minds settled about what it says?

Though it has become a sort of catchphrase for evangelical Christianity, this is a horrible method for understanding the bible. Fundamentally, it errs in breaking what I believe to be very first and most important rule of biblical exegesis (or explanation): taking context seriously. It's a dishonor to the scriptures themselves to take them at their face value. As theologian Karl Barth once said, "I take the bible too seriously to read it literally."

You absolutely cannot read the bible 2,000 years divorced from the original culture, language, and tradition it was written into and pretend to understand it the way it was meant to be understood!

What is really being said with this is, "I think this is what the bible says, I believe *I'm right,* and so I don't have to listen to your dumb ideas!"

The bible is a difficult book. You can't understand it by itself. Instead, it's important to take the time and humbly come before the scriptures with respect, studying carefully what they mean. We far too often read the bible with a preconceived idea of what it's about. However, if we are to be faithful to the bible we must come humbly before it without any such preconceptions.

In marketing they often say that "content it king". But in biblical studies one might likewise say, "*context is king*". Taking the bible seriously means taking the time to study the language, history, and current events that surrounded its original publication. Context is crucial to understanding the original intent of the biblical authors, and what we can learn from them today. Who is this passage written to? What purpose did the author have in mind? What sort of language is being used? These are crucial questions we must address every time we approach the bible if we are to be faithful to its witness.

So when someone says to me, "The rapture is a plain biblical fact", I wonder where in the world they got such an idea. Because frankly, statements like this make me cringe. Calling something a "plain biblical fact" is, in my eyes, just code for lazy exegesis. In fact there are very few things I would ever call a "plain biblical fact". And even then I would only do so after careful study and reflection.

The bible is a complex, sometimes contradictory ? REALLY ? book written by many different individuals from many different periods of time. Only after careful study can we claim to know what it's about. Basing an argument on the assertion that something is a "clear biblical fact" shows a lack of study and a generally lazy approach to truth.

In this chapter I hope to show, through a careful study of 1 Thessalonians 4, why I have concluded that the rapture is scripturally unfounded.

But before we jump into the scriptures themselves let's establish this "golden rule" of interpreting the bible:

We cannot make any judgements about a text until we have studied its context. (Context is king!) This includes studying the language used (including metaphors, figures of speech, and individual word studies), the culture in which it was written, the history surrounding its writing, and the preceding and proceeding passages surrounding the text. Only *after* the context has been studied can we accurately make any judgements about what the text is saying to us today.

Looking at the Text

There are several scriptures often used to back up the rapture. Although, there is only one that I've found to be truly crucial in defending it. This is 1 Thessalonians 4:17. Every other scripture used to support the rapture is based on the assumption that this verse proves the rapture. I have found that this is the only verse that offers any sort of direct support for the rapture, and that all other verses often used are interpreted in its light.[1] So in order to cut the tree down at its root we'll start by dismantling this prime "proof-text".

First, read the verse itself: "Then we who are alive, who are left, will be caught up together with them in the clouds to meet the Lord in the air, and so we will always be with the Lord." (1 Thes. 4:17, ESV)

Rapture theorists are especially interested in the phrase, "We will be caught up together…in the clouds to meet the Lord in the air." It becomes clear with this why this verse is the prime text often used. It seems to say, upon first reading, that we fly up into the sky and meet Jesus. That at His return He will rapture Christians out of this earth.

But there is actually a lot more going on here than meets the eye. There are several clever literary devices Paul is using to illustrate a point. Yet these have often been misunderstood by the careless observer. Without taking context seriously, the

---

[1] Matthew 24 is a good example of a text with the rapture injected into it because of this verse. In Chapter 7 we'll spend time examining that chapter, but it's important to see that 1 Thes. 4 is the only text that *directly* offers any kind of support for the rapture. In Matt. 24 there is only evidence injected into the text, not taken from the text itself.

rapture seems plain in this verse. But let's dig into it a little more and see if that's really the case.

First, let me give you this verse again in conjunction with the whole passage (from v. 13-17):

> (13) But we do not want you to be uninformed, brothers, about those who are asleep, that you may not grieve as others do who have no hope. (14) For since we believe that Jesus died and rose again, even so, through Jesus, God will bring with him those who have fallen asleep. (15) For this we declare to you by a word from the Lord, that we who are alive, who are left until the coming of the Lord, will not precede those who have fallen asleep. (16) For the Lord himself will descend from heaven with a cry of command, with the voice of an archangel, and with the sound of the trumpet of God. And the dead in Christ will rise first. (17) Then we who are alive, who are left, will be caught up together with them in the clouds to meet the Lord in the air, and so we will always be with the Lord. (ESV)

Context

Who is "them"? In verse seventeen Paul says we "will be caught up together with *them* in the clouds..." This cannot be the "we" referred to in this sentence. There is a clear distinction between the "we" who are caught up and the "them" who the "we" meets in the air. So who is "them"?

If we read verse seventeen alone, we cannot answer this question. But once we see the whole picture that Paul is painting from verses 13-17 we have a crystal clear answer. Look at verses fourteen and fifteen, which both use the phrase, "Those who have fallen asleep". This is the "them" referred to by Paul in verse seventeen. It is a clear reference to the dead. We know this because Paul uses the same phrase elsewhere to mean those who have died. It therefore points towards the resurrection as a part of the final coming of Christ.

But why does this matter? Because this reveals Paul's point. He is writing about the resurrection of the dead, of those who have "fallen asleep". By linking together the death and resurrection of Jesus Christ with those who have fallen asleep (v. 14), Paul is saying what he has often said before. In Christ we have died and in Christ we are looking forward to the resurrection to come. This is one of Paul's central teachings found in the New Testament. For example, see Romans 6:3-10, Colossians 3:3-4, and 1 Corinthians 15:12-28.

The early church believed that since God raised Jesus Christ from the dead the end of the world had come. But more importantly, that God was making all things new. (See 2 Cor. 5:14-21.) This is the promise of our resurrection in Christ. In Christ we have died and in Christ we now live, and when He comes again we eagerly expect a glorious resurrection like His. For this reason two of the most important Creeds in Christian history, the Nicene Creed and the Apostles Creed, both declare that we are looking forward to the resurrection of the dead and to life in the world to come. This, traditionally and scripturally, is the Christian hope for the future.

Paul is not describing the rapture in this verse. Instead, his theme is the resurrection. Verse fourteen sets the precedent with this phrase: "For since we believe that Jesus died and rose again…" The context Paul is speaking to is of Jesus' resurrection. His resurrection is the pattern for our resurrection to come. This is a common theme for Paul, one we find all throughout the New Testament.

In verse seventeen Paul uses colorful, Old Testament imagery to describe the indescribable, to describe the resurrection. He borrows from three different sources for this. First, from the story of Moses' decent down the mountain bearing the Torah (the trumpet sounding). And second, from Daniel 7, in which the people of God are vindicated over their enemies by being raised up to sit with God in glory. And finally, with the image of an emperor visiting a colony whose citizens joyfully come out to meet him "in the air". These three allusions have been misunderstood by rapture theorists to mean something entirely different than what Paul intended. But they all tell of a public resurrection which is to come, and not of some spiritual, secret rapture.[2]

Poor Paul, with his brilliant understanding of Old Testament imagery, uses his memory bank of allusions to help describe the indescribable. But he has been horribly misunderstood by rapture theorists

---

[2] The link between Paul and these images was first brought to my attention in an essay by Scholar N. T. Wright entitled "A Farewell to the Rapture". See recommended reading.

ever since. Misunderstanding this passage, with Paul's carefully chosen imagery, has single-handedly created the rapture theory.

A Word Study

A simple word study of this passage also brings out Paul's emphasis on the resurrection. The word in verse seventeen for "sky" is the Greek word *aēr*. This word is used only seven times in the New Testament. Of those seven verses only in this verse from 1 Thessalonians and another from Ephesians is *aēr* used in an allegorical sense.[3] Every other passage uses *aēr* to mean simply the air around us, the lower atmosphere. The official definition of *aēr* is simply our earthly atmosphere, "particularly the lower and denser air as distinguished from the higher and rarer air."[4]

---

[3] Ephesians 2:2. Paul uses "air" in reference to the "prince and power of the air". As an allusion to satan, this is also clearly not a reference to heaven. Satan has no dominion over "heaven", but he does have power over the "air", that is, this earthly domain.

[4] http://www.biblestudytools.com/Lexicons/Greek/grk.cgi?numbers=109&version=nas

This word is purposefully free from any sort of heavenly connotations. It is about the air around us now, the atmosphere of earth. Nothing in this word could lead us to imagine that "sky" is anything other than our earthly sky. Paul very easily could have used the word *ouranós*, which means more precisely "heaven". And *ouranós* is the word rapture theorists often assume Paul has used. But in reality *aēr* is used, indicating the lower atmosphere of the two. Paul is not saying that we meet the Lord in heaven, in the *ouranós*. He has written that we meet the Lord in this atmosphere, here on earth, in the *aēr*.

This word study shows that Paul is not talking about a mystical rapture from earth to heaven. Instead, He is describing the raising up of the dead to life. We meet the dead again in the "air", that is in the atmosphere of a new earth. We are raised to life, to this atmosphere, not raptured off to heaven. The difference in these words, and Paul's deliberate choice of *aēr* over *ouranós* proves this point.

The rest of this passage uses the metaphorically rich language we just discussed. With the cloud referring to a prophecy in Daniel 7, and the trumpet referring to Moses' decent down the mountain. Both allusions give no support for the rapture either.

It is clear with Paul's careful use of *aēr* for sky, that this is not a metaphor for heaven but for earth. It is used to emphasize the hope we have in the resurrection to come. While the passage does contain several metaphorical images, "sky" is not one of them. *Aēr* is a statement about the air around us now, and further proof that Paul's theme is the resurrection and not the rapture.

Historically and Culturally

Paul concludes by saying why he wrote these things. "Therefore encourage one another with these words." The truth of Christ's resurrection and our resurrection to come at His return is a matter of great joy and comfort. The resurrection means that *this* is where the world is heading. It is not heading for a catastrophic event in which millions—if not billions!—of individuals will be tortured while others escape away into the heavens. The world is heading for a beautiful, hopeful resolve in which Christ will raise the dead and the Kingdom of God will reign (see Rev. 21-22).

The belief in a God who willingly raptures some, but leaves the mass of humanity to die and suffer is in no way a comforting belief. Such a belief contradicts the goodness and love of God. As Jürgen Moltmann has written, "A God who only waits to 'rapture' Christian crews from their aircraft so that the aircraft crashes and thousands of persons are killed cannot be a God whom one can trust. Rather that is the wicked idol of a pathological contempt of the world."[5]

The rapture steals hope. Paul wrote to encourage believers, to give hope for the resurrection to come. For the early Christian community, the resurrection meant the beginning of a new world. It meant hope. The historical evidence for this is abundant and undeniable, as most early Christian texts support this emphasis. In the early church, the resurrection was understood as an eschatological (end-times) event. They expected the imminent end of the world and the coming reign of God. It is this hope that Paul is speaking to in 1 Thessalonians 4. Because of this well documented belief shared by most in the early church, it's highly unlikely that Paul wrote of anything other than the resurrection.

---

[5] From the following article: https://web.archive.org/web/20040109155453/http://portland.indymedia.org/en/2002/12/39264.shtml

I firmly feel that any belief that steals hope for the future is a demonic belief. God is the God of hope, not of dread. The rapture is incongruent with such a God, and Paul emphasize this with these words.

Other Voices

What do some of the greatest minds of Christendom have to say about this verse? After two millennia of studying the bible, do any of the great church teachers agree with rapture theorists?

Before the 19th century, no church teacher ever taught the rapture. Nor did any commentator interpret 1 Thes. 4 the way rapture theorists do today. For 1,800 years of church history 1 Thes. 4 was understood as a passage about the resurrection, not the rapture.

John Calvin is among the many respected theologians who never taught the rapture. Calvin writes clearly in his commentary on this passage that, "[Paul] now briefly explains the manner in which believers will be raised up from death." He makes absolutely no mention of this mythical rapture idea, but saw clearly that Paul here is speaking only of the resurrection to come.

Modern scholars also agree that this text is about the resurrection. N.T. Wright teaches that Paul is not speaking of the rapture. Instead, he writes, "Paul's description of Jesus' reappearance in 1 Thessalonians 4 is a brightly colored version of what he says in two other passages, 1 Corinthians 15:51-54 and Philippians 3:20-21: At Jesus' 'coming' or 'appearing,' those who are still alive will be 'changed' or 'transformed' so that their mortal bodies will become incorruptible, deathless. This is all Paul intends to say in Thessalonians, but here he borrows imagery—from biblical and political sources—to enhance his message. Little did he know how his rich metaphors would be misunderstood two millennia later."[6]

The subject of the following chapter will be this lack of historical precedence. The fact is that the rapture is a brand new idea for Christianity. But it helps to point out here that for most of church history 1 Thes. 4 has been understood as a text about the resurrection. The rapture is nowhere to be found in the teachings of the church on this verse.

---

[6] From an essay entitled "Farewell to the Rapture", published August 2001. See recommended sources for more.

Conclusions

All other passages used to proof-text the rapture are nullified in the light of this study. In chapter seven I will deal more with another important scripture: Matthew 24 and its parallel texts. But as I've said, I believe 1 Thessalonians 4 is the chief scripture often used to support the rapture. Other scriptures do not deal directly with the rapture, but rapture theorists imply they do in the light of this text.

Often when a scripture is misused to "prove" the rapture it is in the same way that 1 Thes. 4 has been misused. Rapture theorists mistake the rapture for the resurrection in their biblical exegesis. For example, I've read rapture theorists who have even tried to use 1 Cor. 15:52 to prove the rapture! This is despite the fact that the text itself says, "the dead shall be raised…" This verse is without a doubt talking about the resurrection to come. Rapture theorists often inject their preconceived conclusions into a text, and call it proof. But I believe 1 Thes. 4 is the only "direct" passage that might be used. But since I have shown that this text offers no proof for the rapture, then the rapture itself must be counted false. The rapture is not a "clear biblical fact". To continue to claim so would be to ignorantly ignore the brightest minds in Christendom, along with carefully documented studies of this verse.

Even if my exegesis of this passage is wrong, it is still only one verse. If the rapture is such an essential doctrine, then why are there so few references to it in the bible? The bible simply does not contain a belief in the rapture. To then take it as a concrete fact and claim it with absolute certainty is a disastrous and unfaithful error to make. There is simply no precedence in the scriptures to support a belief in the rapture.

2: Historically Absent

In recent years I've come to appreciate more and more old things. Old books, old music, and sometimes old ways of thinking. There is just something that feels right when you immerse yourself in that which has survived the brutal test of time. There is a beautiful richness in old things that you just don't find in what's new. When I read Shakespeare, for example, I know I read in solidarity with a community of critics, scholars, school-boys, poets, and enthusiasts from all times and places. Old things last for a reason.

In Christianity the same is true. We have a rich and fascinating history. For centuries the church fought and developed what we know today as orthodox theology. From the early heresies of the gnostics, or of Arius, who was triumphantly defeated by the clever Athanasius, to the many councils, creeds, and declarations—our history is full of a battle for the truth. What we believe today has been fought for, and quite literally even bled for. It's a shame that we often don't study this history as much as we should. There are great treasures of knowledge and wisdom stored high in stockpiles down in our collective Church basement. It's foolish to ignore such a rich history.

The rapture, however, is strangely absent from this history. Despite its asserted importance, it is completely missing from the history of the church. For me, this is a major reason why it must be forgotten and left behind as just another heresy. When we talk about the rapture we are talking about a brand new idea. Both scripture and tradition weigh heavily against it.

No Church father, or doctor ever taught the rapture. Neither Augustine, Athanasius, Ambrose, Irenaeus, Basil, Tertullian, Origen, the Gregory's, Cyril, John Chrysostom, Justin Martyr, Jerome, or Hilary taught it. Nor was it taught in the middle ages or in the reformation. Neither Aquinas, Anselm, Abelard, Calvin, Luther, or Zwingli taught it. Nor do any of the important modern theologians teach it. Neither Barth, Bonhoeffer, Bultmann, Moltmann, Pannenberg, the Torrance's, Tillich, Schleiermacher, Wright, or the Niebuhr's ever taught or currently teach it. The rapture is absent from the greatest minds of the church, past and present.

This is an absolute, proven fact: the rapture is a modern invention.

And while this doesn't necessarily make it false, it does put it up against a large question mark. If 2,000 years of church history has not taught such a belief, then who are we to teach it? If the greatest minds in Christendom never taught it, isn't it brazen of us to assert it as absolute truth?

The rapture is a new idea for the church. It first came on the scene in 1830(!), invented by a man named John Darby. No theologian before that time ever taught it. The rapture was only taken seriously after Darby. For 1,800 years the church confessed their faith instead in the resurrection, not the rapture.

So was Darby right? Did the church miss it for 1,800 years, and we're just coming to see it today?

It's possible. It certainly doesn't mean that what is new is wrong.

But it is a strong case against its validity. As Robert Cameron has written: "Surely, a doctrine that finds no exponent or advocate in the whole history and literature of Christendom, for eighteen hundred years after the founding of the Church—a doctrine that was never taught by a Father or Doctor of the

Church in the past—that has no standard Commentator or Professor of the Greek language in any Theological School until the middle of the Nineteenth century, to give it approval, and that is without a friend, even to mention its name amongst the orthodox teachers or the heretical sects of Christendom—such a fatherless and motherless doctrine, when it rises to the front, demanding universal acceptance, ought to undergo careful scrutiny before it is admitted and tabulated as part of the faith once for all delivered unto the saints."[7]

In this book I hope to show that the rapture has a large burden of proof standing against it. There are far more reasons *not* to believe in it than to believe. If you still choose to believe despite this fact, that would be your choice. But consider this a warning. Belief in the rapture goes against the teachings of the church for two millennium.

In the last chapter I showed that the scriptures are silent about the rapture. The verses often used in support of it are used in error. There is no proof to be found in the pages of scripture.

In this chapter I will briefly explain the history of the rapture. This will show the utter lack of any

---

[7] Scriptural Truth About The Lord's Return, page 72-73

historical precedence for its acceptance. Theology is a communal endeavor. It is preformed in the community of the church. This includes all those who have gone before us. It is a serious position to take, then, to say that Darby is right and he saw what 1,800 years of great church theologians have failed to see. And it's highly doubtful that this is so.

Inventing the Rapture

John Darby invented the rapture in the 19th century. No one really knows how or where he got the idea for it. He simply made it up. Timothy P. Weber writes, "…historians are still trying to figure out how or where Darby got it… Probably, we may have to settle for Darby's own explanation. He claimed that the doctrine virtually jumped out of the pages of Scripture once he accepted and consistently maintained the distinction between Israel and the church."[8]

Mostly based upon 1 Thes. 4:17, Darby said he discovered the rapture in 1830 while reading that passage. Ironically though, while rapture theorists try

---

[8] *Living in the Shadow of the Second Coming: American Premillennialism,* P. 21-22

to argue an earlier date, the denomination Darby himself created boasts his discovery as a new discovery for the church.

John Darby was the founder of the Plymouth Brethren. In their statement of faith they claim that Darby discovered this doctrine in 1830, and that before Darby this doctrine was not taught anywhere.[9] This shows by their own admission that Darby was the first to teach the rapture. No Creed, Catechism, or Statement of Faith included the rapture before 1830.

After Darby, the rapture grew in acceptance through the popularity of several resources. The first was the inclusion of the rapture theory into The Scofield Reference Bible. Originally published in 1909, The Scofield Reference Bible was and remains still a popular bible designed to aid individuals in studying the scriptures. It included many annotations and introductions to help readers gain insight into the text. Before the end of World War II, this bible sold over two million copies. It was with the popularity of this bible that the rapture become a common doctrine.

---

[9] See: The Theological Contributions of the Brethren FAQ #16

Additionally, in recent times, Tim LaHaye and Jerry B. Jenkins' *Left Behind* series is perhaps the best known cause of the rapture's acceptance. Though works of fiction, these books promote the rapture as an undeniable biblical truth. *The Left Behind* series of books have taught countless millions to believe the rapture. By asserting the doctrine as truth, it has found stable ground in the theology of America. With the release of *Left Behind* movies it became even more so. The rapture has turned into a bonafide American doctrine. Statistics show that a startling 41% of Americans believe in a literal rapture.[10]

The church is experiencing some serious theological-whiplash! After no mention of the rapture for over 1,800 years, suddenly, in the last 130 years, 41% of Americans believe it. It is mind-boggling to go from that to this in such a short time. Such blind acceptance of this doctrine points to its fad-like popularity. And hopefully, to its eventual fad-like departure. May it go as quickly as it came.

Though it is interesting to consider just how this rapid acceptance took place. Why is it that most now believe in this doctrine despite its lack of credibility? If we think of the rapture like a business, it is like a

---

[10] Pew Research Center

start-up business. Any good financial advisor would be quick to tell you how absolutely foolish it is to invest your life savings into a start up. It's a very bad idea! The youngness of this doctrine alone is reason enough to question its validity. So why in the world would anyone stake their whole life on it as an absolute fact?

The rapture is a *baby* of a doctrine, and should be treated accordingly. If a newborn child started talking gibberish, as babies often do—"gaabba pada dado poo!"—it wouldn't make much sense for me to take the words of that baby and claim that they are the words of a philosophical genius, and therefore contain the meaning of life, and the answer to all the worlds problems. Nor would it be reasonable for me to spend my life deciphering the cryptic talk of this *infant.* But sadly many Christians today are taking this childish rapture doctrine *far too seriously.*

Objections: Ephraim the Syrian

The only objection a rapture theorist may give is to claim that Ephraim the Syrian taught the rapture before Darby. Ephraim the Syrian was an important 4th century deacon of the church. If he in fact taught it, then there is some historical basis for its teaching. However, there are several problems with such an argument.

First of all, even if Ephraim taught the rapture, he wasn't taken seriously. If he is the *only* example theorists can find, that's a poor showing for the rapture. One obscure text proves almost nothing. When rapture theorists use Ephraim to show that the rapture has a historical basis before Darby, they actually *disprove* themselves in the process. Because an obscure reference to the rapture only proves either one of two things. First, that the text has been misinterpreted and really isn't about the rapture. Or second, that Ephraim actually taught the rapture, but everyone thought it was too ridiculous of an idea to take seriously. So whether Ephraim taught the rapture or not is irrelevant. Both scenarios lead not to more proof for the rapture, but proof against it.

And furthermore, if we look at the quote itself, it becomes even clearer. An argument for the rapture cannot be found if you read carefully. If you are desperately searching for quotes to back up your made-up doctrine, then by all means this obscure quote is proof. But for anyone willing to do even the most basic research, it's difficult to argue that the text has anything to do with the rapture. It has been misused to prove the rapture, but in context it describes the resurrection.

The text itself is not worth repeating. But if you want to read it for yourself, I'm sure a simple internet search will find it rather quickly. The main reason it's not worth repeating though is, like many other internet-based quotes, it is a misquote. Most scholars agree that Ephraim the Syrian never even wrote it to begin with. Instead, its authorship has been dated as late as the 8th century. It was written four hundred years after Ephraim's death, by someone writing under his name. It is a "Pseudo-Ephraim" text. Rapture theorists have mistranslated and misinterpreted it to prove the rapture. But all along it is a faulty source to quote. It's a radical stretch on their part. And in a way it reveals their utter desperation, when attempting to prove themselves through such unfounded sources. They are grasping at straws because that's all they have to grasp at. The rapture is absent from the history of the church. It is absent from the scriptures. Obscure, out of context, mistranslated, and misinterpreted passages are all they have to piece together their "doctrine".

This shows that there is no historical evidence supporting the rapture before Darby. It also shows that anyone trying to prove the rapture must go to extreme lengths to do so.

Conclusions

Classically speaking, truth is true for the community of the church whenever it is scripturally accurate and historically founded. I have, in these first two chapters, put the rapture at the mercy of both tests. It has faired poorly!

The scriptures offer no basis for the rapture. The long history of the Christian church offers no basis either. It is therefore an unfounded doctrine with little to show for itself. Individuals who claim the dire importance of the rapture do so in spite of its questionability. Isn't this why they resort to such out-of-context texts and obscure passages? The way rapture theorists talk you'd think the bible is full of proof, but it isn't.

The rapture is a made up, mythological doctrine with almost no evidence to prove otherwise.

These two reasons should be more than enough to drop the rapture as false. Let's write it off for the rest of church history as just another heresy long forgotten.

In the following chapters I hope to take a different approach in disproving the rapture. By using philosophical, logical, and practical reasoning I hope to show even more why the rapture is worth leaving behind for good.

3: Escapism

The Lord created the world and He called it *good*. Dietrich Bonhoeffer once said that, "Only he who loves the earth and God in the same breath can believe in the Kingdom of God." And is he right? Are we supposed to love the world? And I don't mean just those who live in it, but the actual earth itself?

The rapture takes the bountiful gift of God's good earth and turns it into a temporary, soon-to-be-destroyed place we just can't wait to escape. If you've ever watched Star Trek, the classic phrase "beam me up, Scotty!" summarizes perfectly what most believe will take place. The world will fall apart, creation destroyed, and we Christians will be the lucky ones who get teleported out of here.

But is this God's plan for the earth He calls *good?* To escape all earthly life and trade it for a mystical heavenly existence?

This, I feel, is one of the most detrimental by-products of the rapture doctrine. It cultivates an unhealthy disdain for earthly existence, and an unhealthy desire to escape it. But God did not create the world to one day destroy it. God created the world, called it good, and will not quickly abandon the work of His hands.

Escapism is absent from the scriptures and the tradition of the church. The early believers weren't looking for a quick way out of this "mess" of a planet. Instead, they worked towards *building something here.* They expected eagerly the return of Jesus, but that expectation never lead to escapism. Instead, they worked towards bettering this world here and now by taking care of the poor, helping those in need, and preaching the good news of God's favor.

We could also look at it like this. Why did the early church suffer persecution from the Roman Empire? If their message was about some other-world called heaven, why attack it? Why was the church martyred, incarcerated, and tortured for preaching? If their gospel was about *the next world* and not *this* one, then why would the Roman Empire care to outlaw it? A message about a "spiritual" Kingdom does not merit such widespread Christian persecution. But that was not the message they preached. The church was not persecuted for preaching heaven. They were persecuted for preaching the Kingdom of God. They boldly proclaimed that Jesus Christ is Lord. They proclaimed the reign of God on this earth, not merely in some distant place. Theirs was a message just as human and earthly as their crucified and risen Messiah. As such, many early believers gave their lives to proclaim it.

The rapture takes the emphasis away from this world and places it into the next. But for the early Christians this was unthinkable. They were deeply interested in advancing the Kingdom here on this earth. Our "escape this world and go to heaven" gospel is not the true gospel passed down to us from the first apostles. Theirs was a message of Kingdom come.

Art, Culture, and All the Ways We've Fallen Behind

I believe art is one of the most powerful communities in the world because it is a timeless community. I was lucky enough to visit Rome with my wife this past autumn. Rome is a beautiful city with such a rich history and culture. As someone who loves art, I enjoyed most of all visiting Michelangelo's fantastic Sistine Chapel. It was a life-changing experience. To stand in the presence of one of the greatest masterpieces of all time, in a room where countless others have stood to take part in its magnificence, was amazing. In fact, viewing all the great artwork from the Vatican's collection was a delight. The wealth of tremendous art there is overwhelming.

But why build the Sistine Chapel, or paint a masterpiece, or write a play, or compose a symphony if very soon it will all be destroyed and we'll disappear from this earth? Why invest your life making something beautiful, if it won't last for more than a few years?

The Christian church used to be on the forefront of creating great art, music, and literature. Many of the greatest masterpieces of all time are the by-product of church commissioning or influence. But when you ask the same of today's church, you'll sadly see we have fallen far behind. The Christian church today is slow to progress in the world of art.

Art is one of the most human endeavors one could take up. It is purely an act of creation from the heart. As such it is an important part of this world—

the most essential, I would argue. But we have become increasingly irrelevant to it. Escapism has led us to falling far, far behind. We really don't create beautiful things as a community anymore.[11] Instead, we produce sad parodies of creativity.

The rapture has stolen away our sense of a future, and so we spend little time building one. This is why I'm bringing up art. Art is timeless. And we have become a short-sighted people. We have gone into hiding, merely waiting for escape.

We have lost influence by losing our hope. A wise man once said, "He who has the most hope has the most influence."[12] We have lost our hope, that is, our sense of a future, and so our influence has gone with it. We used to be beacons of hope for this world, as children of "the God of Hope", but the rapture has stolen it away. We no longer believe that great things are on the horizon. We have given up on this world and let a pessimistic doctrine run rampant.

And so this isn't just about art. Art is just one field we've neglected. Bill Bright made popular the

---

[11] With some exceptions—thankfully! Arvo Pärt, the Orthodox composer, comes to my mind right away.

[12] I can't give you an exact citation for this, but I believe it was Bill Johnson who said it.

idea of the "seven mountains of influence". These include the realms of business, government, media, arts and entertainment, education, the family, and religion. If the church would focus less on the next world and more on this one, we may once again become influencers in each realm. But as long as we expect a rapture, it is unlikely that we will.

The fact is *this world has left us behind* while we stare at the clouds, waiting. We are called to bring the Kingdom to this earth, to preach the message of God's reign, that "Jesus is Lord". We mustn't become hopeless escapists. We must once again become deeply interested, as the early church was, in *this* world.

Martin Luther once said, "The Christian shoemaker does his duty not by putting little crosses on the shoes, but by making good shoes." We have forgotten that God is interested in this world. The rapture has affected our ability to give witness to the goodness of God here and now. When we fixate on a mythical escape to the next world more than life in this world, we fail to preach the gospel. We are called to build the kingdom here. But we are expecting to fly away to some other place—as if the Kingdom is *elsewhere,* and not here. The rapture doctrine has made us short-minded.

Escapism is a dangerous mindset. The rapture must be left behind because it turns us into escapists. We cannot afford to be short-sighted, selfish, and quick to abandon this planet. We must once again take up the call to invest in the future, building with longterm vision in mind.

Gnosticism

One of the first heresies the Christian church faced was gnosticism. The gnostics were those who believed in a philosophy of escapism. They believed that this world was ruled by an evil power, and therefore that earthly existence was grotesque and corrupt. They consequently sought to transcend this gross, earthly world for a pure, spiritual one. Their philosophy manifested itself in two different ways. One being the absolute abstinence of all earthy pleasure. The other being the absolute indulgence in pleasure. Though both responses come from the idea that this world is evil and we must seek a higher spiritual reality beyond it.[13]

St. Irenaeus writes about gnosticism in his important 2nd century work *Against Heresies.* "[Gnosticism] held matter to be a deterioration of spirit, and the whole universe a depravation of the Deity, and taught the ultimate end of all being to be the overcoming of the grossness of matter and the return to the Parent-Spirit, which return they held to be inaugurated and facilitated by the appearance of some God-sent Savior."

Escapism and the rapture doctrine are not new heresies. The early church fought tirelessly against such a belief. They fought to preserve the message of Jesus as one which values this earth. For the early church this was a Christological issue, primarily. Because if our world is inherently gross and corrupt, then God could not enter into it. God could not become a man. Escapism in this way threatens to

---

13 It also lead to the dangerous belief that Jesus Christ did not come in the flesh, but as a spirit. Scripture verses such as 1 Tim. 6:20-21, 1 John 4:2, and Col. 2:8 directly oppose gnosticism.

undo the incarnation itself. Because why would God become man if the earth is temporary?[14]

The incarnation is God's affirmation of earthly life and the earth itself. It is His *Yes* to our world. He became a man to redeem mankind and in so doing recaptured the blessing earthly life was always intended to be. We mustn't be quick to abandon this earth, or forget that life here is a tremendous blessing. The rapture devalues life on planet earth in favor of escaping to another, more spiritual realm. Yet God has declared in Jesus an eternally affirming *Yes* to human existence—a Yes to flowers, trees, sunshine, cupcakes, wine, chocolate, mountains, puffy clouds, human bodies, and all the marvelous days the earth so graciously has given us. We would be foolish, then, to call evil what God has called good, to say *no* to what He has said *Yes* to.

Robert F. Capon, author and theologian, once went so far as calling God, "The Ultimate Materialist". Saying, "There is a habit that plagues many so-called spiritual minds: they imagine that matter and spirit are somehow at odds with each other and that the right course for human life is to

---

[14] This is why Revelation tells of a new heaven and a new *earth*. Creation will be made new, not destroyed in the end.

escape from the world of matter into some finer and purer (and undoubtably duller) realm. To me, that is a crashing mistake—and it is, above all, a theological mistake. Because, in fact, it was God who invented dirt, onions and turnip greens; God who invented human beings, with their strange compulsion to cook their food; God who, at the end of each day of creation, pronounced a resounding 'Good!' over his own concoctions. And it is God's unrelenting love of all the stuff of this world that keeps it in being at every moment. So, if we are fascinated, even intoxicated, by matter, it is no surprise: we are made in the image of the Ultimate Materialist."[15]

God has blessed life on planet earth. It would be foolish to promote a teaching that cultivates contempt for His creation. We're not put on earth to one day leave it behind. This world is our home. The second coming will not bring the destruction of this earth, but the fulfillment of creation. "Behold! I am making all things new."

---

[15] From *The Supper of the Lamb*

4: A Fear-Driven Philosophy

If the rapture is such a logically inconsistent and irresponsible belief, as I claim here, then why have so many taken to it as fact? Why, despite evidence to the contrary—scriptural, historical, or logical—have many flocked to the rapture like it is their shelter from a storm?

A primary driver, I believe, is fear.

When I first began writing about the rapture one of the common responses I received proves this point. I was often told, "Well, what if you're wrong?"

Well, so what if I am? The implied logic essentially says that it's better to live in fear, even if it's unnecessary to do so, than it is to think critically about the validity of the rapture. But what if we reversed this line of reasoning?

The philosopher Blaise Pascal offers a famous wager about belief in God, which is often called Pascal's Wager. Simply, he posited that all people bet with their lives either that God exists or not. He argued that it is in the best interest of an individual to behave as if God exists, because the risk of being wrong is far less than the alternative. If God does exist, and therefore the possibility of eternal damnation exists too, then the risk of not believing is a far greater risk than the risk of believing. Essentially meaning that belief in God is safer than atheism given the possibility of eternal damnation. Therefore it's best to believe in God, and practice some sort of theism.

If we take a similar line of thinking, I too could postulate a wager in regards to the rapture theory.

A rapture-believing individual has more to lose than a non-rapture-believer. If I am wrong and the rapture is true, the only loss I suffer is being wrong (and surprised) because the rapture actually happened. But if the rapture is false and the rapture-believing individual is wrong, then the rapture-believer would have spent his or her life afraid of this catastrophic event that never took place. Furthermore, the rapture-believer would also be charged with spreading this fear and a harmful vision of what God is like by teaching the rapture as fact. Therefore, it is far more dangerous to believe in the rapture than it is not to. It is in your best interest, therefore, even if there is a possibility I am wrong (which I am not so naive as to say there isn't), to disbelieve rather than to believe in the rapture theory. You will save both yourself and those around you from a fear-mongering belief of doom and gloom. Radical hope for the coming Kingdom is a far better alternative.

When I used to believe in the rapture it was mostly because I never took the time to question it's validity. And I never questioned it because I was too terrified of it to even consider it's falsehood. This is the nature of fear. It clouds your ability to think critically. Fear psychologically gives you a mindset of either "fight or flight". That is certainly not the state of mind we're to be in to make a difference in this world. But it's interesting to examine this in many Christian end-times camps.

You may find a fight or flight mindset in many churches today. Subconsciously I think that many believers, due to their inherited pessimism, have resorted to one or the other.

On one side, Christian Zionists and others like them dedicate themselves to fighting against their selected social scapegoats. Be it Muslims, homosexuals, liberals, or socialists. You'll see these groups portrayed as the "enemy" or cause to fight against. These churches, in the light of their pessimistic world-view, have chosen to fight against the darkness. Sadly though, they often end up fighting against the same people that God loves and supports.

On the other side, many in the church resort to a "flight" mentality. Many Christians have become reclusive to exclusively Christian communities. They limit themselves to fellowship with Christians alone by going only to Christian schools, listening to Christian music, and reading Christian books. A whole sub-culture has been established around this "flight" mentality. But we're not here on planet earth to build a reclusive sub-culture. We're here to influence all cultures with the message of God's favor and love.

The pessimistic worldview of rapture theorists results in a fear-induced "flight or fight" response.

From personal experience, too, I can say that fear was the only reason I believed. I was under the fearful shadow of the worlds imminent demise. I found comfort in reclusion and escapism. The world can be a scary place, and to make sense of it all we try to invent an easy way out. But no such way exists. We are here on planet earth whether we like it or not. We are here to bring the Kingdom of God, and manifest the love He has for all people.

When we examine the logical pros and cons for believing or disbelieving, the results show that it is more favorable to give up the rapture for good. Any belief that is primarily built on fear is a problematic, dangerous belief. We shouldn't listen to fear.

Fear Sells

The underlying philosophy behind the rapture says that the world must get worse and worse before we escape it. This is a large reason why the rapture creates fear. Many will say that it does not, that it is about hope, but in the same breath they will be quick to tell you about the latest bombing, serial killer, or natural disaster, calling these a "sign of the times". There is a clear and undeniable pessimism that goes along with the rapture theory. Because how can one not be afraid when focusing on all that's wrong with the world?

In some extreme cases, the rapture has even caused some to secretly *wish* for disaster and calamity. Why? Because such evil signs hasten the day of the Lord's return and their escape. The early

Christian declaration of hope, "come Lord Jesus, come", becomes, on the lips of a rapture theorists, essentially, "Beam me up, Scotty! Get me out of this mess!"

Fear sells faster in Christian circles than a wildfire spreads across a dry desert. This is especially true when you attach a biblical precedence to your fear-mongering. At the moment, a popular author has claimed that various "blood-moons" seen in the sky during 2015 are harbingers of the end times. The claim is that very soon God will shake the world with a great testing and cause many terrible things to happen. And these sort of books sell like hot-cakes because people are afraid and looking for easy answers. This is all despite the fact that such books are often poorly researched and mocked by well respected scholars.[16]

Anyone who capitalizes on predicting that bad things will happen is a false teacher trying to get rich by scaring people. It is a marketing technique to turn a profit. Plain and simple. History has seen this time and time again with books promising, yet failing to

---

[16] Greg Boyd has a series of videos on his website that disprove these teachings. For more see Recommended Reading.

predict, the end of the world in 1988, 1989, Y2K, 2012, and now 2015. And these examples just scratch the surface of the countless other failed predictions people have given since the rapture theory came into popular existence. If we're to "judge a tree by its fruit", that is, a teaching by its results, or a prediction by its accuracy, then the rapture has shown itself false solely on these failed predictions given by its doomsday "prophets".

The rapture is a belief founded on fear, and fear sells.

I say this not as an outsider looking in, but as someone who once held firmly onto the belief that the rapture would happen in my lifetime. I myself would never have admitted it, but in retrospect I now see that I only believed because I was scared into believing. Anything that uses fear as its primary motivator is a problematic belief. The rapture is no exception.

Alive in the Age of Worry

I'm unashamedly a huge John Mayer fan. I just love his music. Not only is he an incredible guitar player, probably one of the best alive today, but he's also a great song-writer. One of his newer songs I enjoy is called *The Age of Worry*. It's all about living in an age where worrying about everything is common and trying to be something your not is status quo. Lyrics like "make friends with what you are" and "don't be scared to walk alone, don't be scared to like it" make it a lyrically rich song. But one of my favorite lines comes at the end: "Alive in the age of worry... act your age in the age of worry and say, 'worry, why should I care?'"

We may live in an age where everyone, even, and sometimes especially, Christians, are screaming doom and gloom and the end of all things. But we have a reason to say, "worry, why should I care?" in the face of all the fear that runs rampant in this world. Worry may speak to us on a daily basis, but we always have a choice to ignore it.

Any belief, Christian or otherwise, that creates fear is a belief we should quickly leave behind. There are many times throughout the bible where God commands us not to be afraid. When Jesus appears to John in the book of Revelation He says, "Do not be afraid. I am the first and the last, and the living One; and I was dead, and behold I am alive forevermore and I have the keys of death and of hades." (Rev. 1:17 NASB)

Fear is our enemy. "There is no fear in love; but perfect love casts out fear." (1 John 4:18) We may live in the "age of worry", but we mustn't be afraid. The One who is and who was and who is to come is on our side. The rapture is inconsistent with the God of love because it is a belief that spreads fear and a sense of foreboding. We cannot accept a belief that undermines one of the most important facts we know about God: that He is a God of love, a God who *is* love, and therefore a God who is for us. The rapture is incongruent with such a God.

5: The Improving State of the World

Proof is found in the lives of countless thousands who have felt a crippling fear of the rapture. (I would know, I used to be one of them.) You will know a belief by the fruit it produces, and the rapture produces a nasty concoction of fear, hysteria, and foreboding. Such a belief is unfit for the Christian faith.

Foreboding, the feeling that something bad is about to happen, is a side-effect built into the rapture's teaching. It *expects* terrible events to occur —and by terrible I mean catastrophically terrible such as the mass murder of thousands, or the destruction of entire cities. It is an inherently pessimistic belief. By expecting the rapture, one is at once expecting the very worst time in human history. If it was not enough to see that the rapture is scripturally inaccurate and historically absent, I hope you will be convinced in seeing this horrible sense of foreboding it creates. Built into its philosophy of fear is a belief that the world is getting worse every day. Not only is this a horrible, horrible worldview to have, but an inaccurate one. The facts have shown that the world is actually not getting worse, but much, much better. Society is progressively improving in leaps and bounds, and this is good news, something worthy of celebration.

While the rapture is based on a fearful ideology, an ideology of societies decline, that things are getting worse, the facts show the very opposite. The world is getting better.

This chapter will show the statistics of our ever improving world. Contrasted with the rapture, these statistics reveal that the world is not declining as it assumes. Things are getting better. And since things are getting better, a philosophy of doom and gloom can no longer stand.

I'm afraid that many will read these statistics and say they prove nothing. But with eyes of hope may you see the coming Kingdom of God on this earth, the coming reign of justice, and the improving state of our world.

Statistics of an Improving World

It is factually inaccurate to assert that the world is getting worse. Many rapture teachers will say that we are living in dark times, and that it is only going to get darker before the Lord returns. But this ignores the actual facts of our world today. We are living in one of the greatest, most prosperous times of all recorded history. We have less war, more peace, less poverty, more financial stability, less hunger, more justice, and as a whole the lives of people all around the world are improving.

The world is improving more and more each day. Though the rapture relies on a philosophy of doom and gloom, the fact is that our world is getting better.

Don't believe me? Think about it like this. If the world really is getting worse then tell me what time period you'd prefer to live in? Assuming, as rapture theorists do, that there even is a better time to be alive, what time would that be? I honestly doubt when you think it through you could find a time in history better off than we are right now. Because would you really prefer, for example, the impoverished and war stricken early 1900's? Or would you prefer the middle ages, when plagues and disease ran rampant? Or what about the time of Jesus, with the Roman occupation and widespread injustice all throughout the world?

Less than one-hundred years ago women couldn't even vote in the United States. Just over fifty years ago it was acceptable for husbands to commit acts of domestic violence against their children or wives. Before the 1930s, without antibiotics, a simple infection could have killed you. Next time you get the flu, thank God science has progressed enough that a cold won't kill you. Infant mortality is significantly lower now than it was just one-hundred years ago, too. Advances in medicine have made it easier and safer to give birth.

Just think of all the amazing medical breakthroughs that have taken place in the last one-hundred years. Or think of the numerous technological advances that have made our lives easier and safer. There are countless examples of such breakthroughs that show life is improving on planet earth. Would you really like to go back to a time of less health and comfort?

Statistically speaking, the world is less hungry now than it ever has been. In just the last forty years the world hunger rate has dropped by a startling 47%. In 1970 around 25% of the world was hungry, whereas in 2010 a study revealed that only 13% suffered from hunger. While this is in part due to population growth, it still shows a decrease in hunger in relation to population. Hunger is becoming less and less of an issue worldwide.

Our average life expectancy has drastically improved as well. For most of human history the average person was expected to live somewhere between twenty or thirty years old. The World Health Organization now has estimated that the world wide average is seventy-one. We now live on average more than three times longer than anyone else has ever lived before.

Our world is also far more literate than it ever has been before. From 1970 to the early 2000s, global illiteracy fell from 46% to 18%. This means that more people have the ability to learn, grow, and improve themselves through reading.[17]

The fact is that we now live much longer, healthier, easier, more convenient lives than ever before in all recorded history.

Our world is getting better! Rapture theorists and end-time "prophets" are living in a delusional world of their own making. Things are improving.

---

[17] These statistics are recorded in *The Improving State of the World* by Indur Goklany (2007)

Partially due to the sensationalism of media outlets, it's easy to imagine that the world is an ever darkening place. While it's true that bad things do happen, there are also many incredible things happening every day that we simply can't ignore. Every day brilliant scientists are working to discover new cures, better medicine, and more precise tools to help fight against disease. Inventors are finding ways to make our lives safer, and easier. We truly are living in a wonderful time, with many new, exciting things happening around us every single day.

The foreboding beliefs of those who teach the rapture are an unfounded delusion, and proof that the rapture is a corrupt, problematic belief we must be rid of.

The proof of the pudding is in the eating: the facts speak for themselves. The world is not getting worse. It is improving. The rapture, and the foreboding feeling that goes with it, is a plague we must remove from the church. If we live in our delusional fantasy of an ever worsening world, we will fail to see the coming Kingdom of God in human history. We work against God's justice when we desire societies decline into darkness. But we work with God's hopeful return when we look forward to the ever improving state of humanity leading up to the time in which God will make all things new.

6: Literalism (Poor Hermeneutics)

If I had to take the bible one hundred percent literally, as biblical literalists often do to defend the rapture, then I would be forced to take several drastic, illegal measures in my life such as stoning to death any children who disobey their parents (Deuteronomy 21:18-21), or anyone who worships other gods (Leviticus 20). I'd also never let my wife wear jeans again (Deuteronomy 22:5), or speak in any public church meetings (1 Corinthians 14:34). Additionally, I would believe that one day a literal beast with seven heads, ten horns, and ten crowns will actually rise up from the sea with the feet of a bear, the mouth of a lion, and the body of a leopard (Revelation 13).

But that'd be ridiculous.

The fact is absolutely no one reads the bible one hundred percent literally. Yet, rapture theorists will often firmly defend themselves, saying they are merely interpreting the scriptures *literally*. Common scriptures include the aforementioned 1 Thes. 4, alongside Matthew 24, Luke 17, Revelation, Daniel

9, and a few other obscure passages. Rapture theorists wrongly attempt to prove themselves by reading these literally, ignoring the various contextual elements and literary devices implemented by their respective authors. Such literalism is a poor, sloppy hermeneutical principle. And this is not only because it's impossible to be consistently literal with the scriptures, but because it's lazy to ignore context and read the bible at face value all the time, *i.e.* literally.

We've already considered literalism in the rapture theorists interpretation of 1 Thes. 4, and we will talk more about it in the next chapter as we look at Matthew 24. But here I'll present three good reasons why literalism is a flawed method for interpreting scripture.

Three Reasons Why Literalism is Problematic

Reason #1: The bible never supports literalism as an accepted method.

There is an important principle for understanding the bible that in itself undermines the literalists method. That is, we must let the bible interpret itself, whenever possible.

The bible is made up of various books written by several authors who come from many different time periods. These authors have often referenced other books, making the bible a self-referencing text. For example, Paul will often use Old Testament images or prophetic texts to understand what took place in Jesus Christ. The gospel writers did the same by highlighting the various prophecies fulfilled in the life of Christ.

Additionally, Jesus also examined the scriptures, revealing to us how He understood them. Did Jesus read the bible literally? I think the scriptures will show that He did not. And in fact, He did many things when reading the bible that, if done again today, a literalist would quickly call Him a false teacher or a deceiver. A great example for this comes from Luke 4:18-19, 21:

"The Spirit of the Lord is upon me, because He has anointed me to proclaim good news to the poor. He has sent me to proclaim liberty to the captives and recovering of sight to the blind, to set at liberty those who are oppressed, to proclaim the year of the Lord's favor" ...And he began to say to them, "Today this scripture has been fulfilled in your hearing." (ESV)

Jesus went to the temple and read from the book of Isaiah, chapter 61. But Jesus stopped reading *in the middle of a sentence.* He does not finish, as Isaiah does, with "...to proclaim the year of the Lord's favor, *and the day of vengeance of our God."* Jesus takes this passage and purposefully picks what He wishes to exclude from it. If Jesus were a literalist He would be forced to read the whole text because, according to a strictly literal interpretation of the bible, all texts are inherently correct at face value. A literalist would claim that He has purposefully deceived His listeners, and should instead stick to just preaching the literal word of God. But Jesus took a contextual understanding of the scriptures by leaving off the second half of this verse.

Jesus also preformed another contextual re-understanding of the scriptures when He preached the Sermon on the Mount. He would preach, "You've heard it said...But I say to you." This shows that Jesus commonly corrected the Pharisees black-and-white literal understanding of the law with a more contextual understanding that lined up with His Father's will.

You could say that Jesus had this right, being God, but I would argue that He was showing us how to see past the letter of the law to the spirit of the scriptures. He wasn't just God in our flesh trying to impress us, He came to heal us and teach us. Wouldn't He teach us how to read the scriptures, knowing what an important role they'd play in our future life as the church? I think He did. And I also think this is one of Paul's points in Galatians 5 when He discussed the letter and spirit of the law. We are to live by the spirit of the law, and not by the literal, rigid letter of the law.

The bible does not take itself literally. Instead, the bible uses context, both cultural and historical, as a means of witnessing to the Word of God. We cannot then take the bible so literally when it has not taken itself literally.

Reason #2: Many important Christians throughout history did not read the bible literally.

Many literalists would be surprised to know that St. Augustine, one the most influential fathers of the western church, did not believe in a literal seven day period of creation. He believed that God created the world in one single moment, and that the seven day creation account of Genesis does not tell of the literal passing of time. Many other church fathers and great theologians throughout history have taught that the bible is, at times, not a literal book but a figurative or allegorical one (depending on the particular text). Obviously some texts in the bible are literal, but not *all* texts. A skilled interpreter is able to recognize when the bible is using figurative language and when it is not. Literalists fail to make this distinction, and they do so in error.

Reason #3: The bible as a jar of clay.

Paul calls believers "jars of clay" (2 Cor. 4:7) molded by God. God loves to use the weak, fallible lives of human beings to do extraordinary things. He decided to use Moses the murder, David the adulterer, Peter the denier, Thomas the doubter, and Lazarus the dead for marvelous exploits. A life given to God, however inadequate, is a life made extraordinary.

Is the bible itself any different? To say that the bible is in itself a book of ready-made, infallible truths to be taken literally leaves little room for faith. Instead, I think the bible is a "jar of clay" that, in the hands of God, has become something inspired, and trustworthy. It is okay to accept that the bible is a book written by many fallible human beings, which has become the word of God through inspiration. It is a human book. It is also Divinely inspired and breathed upon. It is, like us, a jar of clay that God has molded and ordained for special use. It is not necessarily perfect in itself, but it has become perfect in that God has blessed it to give witness to His Word.

It's okay to see the bible honestly, as a human book. But that absolutely doesn't discredit God's ability to speak His perfect Word through these fallible human words.

And the truth is, even if the bible is a collection of ready-made, infallible truths, we don't actually have access to these original scriptures to begin with. The bible we have today is a copy of a copy written, re-written, and passed down from fallible human beings to other fallible human beings. And these texts have then been translated into hundreds of different versions, one of which you have personally chosen to read. If you take all this into consideration it's hard to take anyone seriously who says they read the bible completely literally. The bible is a jar of clay, molded by God for special use. It is the Word of God, but it is also the word of man. God has taken these texts and He has breathed on them, giving them life. But this doesn't mean we can't be honest about what they really are.

Instead of a book of ready-made, undeniable truths, we must take the bible seriously enough to see it as a jar of clay that God has placed treasures within. We should read it seriously, knowing that it is the inspired word of God, but not literally because we are honest about what it is: a book written by men from different time periods with flaws and cultural limitations influencing their writing.

It shouldn't surprise us that God has given us His word in a book written by a group of less-than-perfect people. He loves to use the "foolish things of the world to shame the wise…the weak things of the world to shame the strong." (1 Cor. 1:27) To take literally the bible is to assume that at face value it is perfect. But to take the bible seriously is to see that, though inspired, it is still a book with limitations. And as such we must take our time to study and understand when figurative language, allegorical allusions, and story telling is being used in the text. When we're honest about what the bible actually is, we can then read it appropriately.

We can also then come to understand what a miracle the bible itself truly is. It was God's choice to use this book of limitations in order to speak His Word that is without limitation. It is a miraculous book for this reason: not because it is inherently special, but because God has chosen it. Just like us. We are not inherently worthy of marvel, yet God has chosen to take our lives and make something magnificent.

Conclusions

Failing to recognize the various literary devices used in the bible is the error rapture theorists often make in their biblical studies. It is frankly an insult to the bible itself to limit the language it uses to only literal interpretations. Thus, with the fall of this method comes the fall of the rapture theory itself.

(I want to clarify here that I highly value the bible. This chapter may leave you with a different conclusion, but I hope you see beyond that. I hope to say that the bible is an incredible book. But it is not an end times code book, or a collection of ready-made truths. It is not God's strong-armed message, it is His *foolish* message. Those who try and take the bible and use it as a big stick to beat people with are missing that point. It is an odd book, but I believe it is God's chosen book to bear the message of Jesus Christ. As such it is the foolish thing that confounds the wise, and the weak thing that puts to shame the strong.)

7: Inconsistent Literalism (Sloppy Hermeneutics)

One of the most significant events for the early church, the first that universally effected all believers, was the destruction of the Jewish temple in AD 70. During this time the city of Jerusalem was destroyed, more than a million Jews were slaughtered, and thousands more were left homeless, hopeless, and afraid. The destruction of the Jewish temple was at once the destruction of what made the Jewish people Jewish. Their culture was nearly demolished with its destruction. This war was more than just a massive loss of life, but also a pointed attacked against the very heart of Jewish culture.

If such an event of equal proportion took place here in America, it'd be beyond devastating. You'd have to imagine not only the mass of our population slaughtered, but the cultural centers of America destroyed. Imagine the very heart of American culture gone in an instant: the Statue of Liberty, the White House, the Pentagon, the national museums, Hollywood, the Golden Gate Bridge, and many other American treasures that define us suddenly destroyed. This was the devastating effect of AD 70 for the Jewish People. It crippled an entire nation. The war waged by the Roman Empire against the Jewish people ended in the near total abolishment of Jewish culture. They attempted and almost succeeded in removing Israel completely from the pages of history.

But this did not take place without God's warning. Jesus warned the Jewish people that very soon this would take place. He warned them of the coming destruction, and it was recorded in the New Testament. If you compare Jesus' words in Matthew 24[18] with historical accounts of Jerusalem's destruction this becomes clear. Jesus' words are precise in predicting what took place. One such account comes from the Jewish historian Josephus. He wrote a book called *The Jewish War* in 75 AD, which chronicles the events that took place.

If we're to understand the scriptures correctly we must take this into consideration. Matthew 24 is written with it in mind. However, rapture theorists have manipulated its careful imagery into supporting

---

[18] Along with Luke 17 and 21, a parallel passage to Matthew 24.

their theory, thus making the words of Jesus fit their agenda. But a study of this text, alongside the historical events of 70 AD, will reveal how dishonest and unfounded the rapture theorists conclusions are.

In the last chapter we talked about how rapture theorists use a problematic method called literalism. It is a method which fails to acknowledge context. In this chapter I hope to do two things. First, to show that Matthew 24 is an example of this literalism. And second, to show that this literalism is inconsistently implemented. Not only do rapture theorists practice this faulty method, they do so inconsistently by picking when to be literal and when not to be.

Jesus predicted the destruction of Jerusalem with a very precise series of statements found in Matthew 24. To undo the damage done by rapture theorists who have taken these predictions wrongly, we will now examine Matthew 24, and parallel texts, alongside historical accounts to understand what was intended.

This Generation

"Truly I say to you, this generation will not pass away until all these things take place." (Matthew 24:34 NASB)

A rapture theorist, due to their preconceived conclusions, simply cannot take this statement literally. And why not? There simply is no indication in the text to show that a "generation" is not a literal generation. Jesus is not speaking figuratively, because the text itself shows no such allusion. But, for a rapture theorist, since this verse, taken literally, contradicts their already predetermined conclusion about what Jesus is saying, simply cannot understand it that way. There is no indication of figurative imagery, nor is there any precedence to show that this generation could mean anything other than a literal generation. Nowhere else in the scriptures, if you do a simple word study, does "this generation" mean anything figurative or allegorical. It is therefore not possible to take it figuratively as rapture theorists do.

Simply speaking then, it is unethical to read your own conclusions into this text. We must read truth *from* the bible not *into* the bible. All signs point to the fact that Jesus actually meant "this generation", as in a literal 30-40 year period of time.

Despite the claim, "the bible says it, I believe it, and that settles it", most rapture theorists will find every way possible to work around this verse. They are therefore inconsistent in their reading of the scriptures, picking and choosing when to read a text at face value and when to read it figuratively. Which, again, isn't necessarily a problem by itself, everyone does this. But it is a problem when you read literally what the bible indicates is figurative (such as 1 Thes. 4 and the Old Testament imagery used), or figuratively what is literal (such as this passage here). The problem with a literal interpretation of the scriptures is not that the bible is always figurative, but that the bible is a mixture of literal and figurative. It takes a careful reading of the text, reading *from* the text not into it, to know when it's one or the other. Rapture theorists, instead, read how they want to read: literally when it gives proof to their theory, or figuratively when it does not.

This text gives context to the rest of what Jesus says in this passage. Since there is no indication of figurative language, we must take Him literally. He is not here speaking of some future occurrence in *our* lifetime, but in the lifetime of His first audience. Therefore He is speaking to what is now history for us, the events of AD 70.

Jesus' Warnings

Josephus was a Jewish historian who wrote about the destruction of Jerusalem in AD 70. His book, *The Jewish War,* gives a detailed account of what took place. When compared with Jesus' statements in Matthew 24 it becomes clear that Jesus was speaking to that event and not to some future event to come. Without knowing this context, or carefully studying these passages, one may very well interpret Jesus' words as an obscure prophecy about the rapture or the end times. However, with this historical context in mind it becomes easy to see that this is an incorrect interpretation. Instead, Matthew 24 is a warning about what took place historically in AD 70.

We'll now go through a few of the warnings given by Jesus and compare them with Josephus' account of 70 AD.

Birds of Prey:

One of the most interesting parallels between what Jesus spoke and what Josephus gave an account of is the statement: "Wherever the corpse is, there the vultures [or eagles] will gather." (V. 28) The Roman empire at the time bore the symbol of a bird of prey. This symbol is known as the *Aquila*. It resembled a large bird, similar to an eagle or a vulture. And according to Josephus' account, when the Romans destroyed Jerusalem they first surrounded the city, cutting the Jews off from any escape. They circled their prey just like a vulture does, and on their shields they wore this symbol.

This bird symbolism is a fascinating example of how direct Jesus' statement is. The bird was the official sign of the Roman army at the time, and Jesus predicts that their prey would soon be destroyed. A first century believer would have easily recognized this statement as a clever allusion to the Roman empire. During the Roman occupation, the Jews undoubtably became familiar with the Roman Aquila. In today's terms this would be like the American image of the donkey and the elephant as symbols of political parties. Just as we today would know exactly what's being referenced with a donkey or elephant, so, in the same way, would the Jewish people have known exactly what Jesus meant by a bird of prey circling its victim.

Women with Children:

The next parallel I want to show is by far the most terrifying, so I'll be brief. Jesus gives a warning to pregnant and nursing mothers in verse nineteen. Josephus gives a grotesque account to parallel. It reads like something straight out of a horror film.

The famine induced by the war was so great that starving, nursing women were said to have murdered, and eaten *their very own children.* This gives us insight into just how terrible this really was for the Jewish people. The absolute vicious nature of this war was so great that its psychological effect caused desperate mothers to go against every instinct they have and find food in their own family. In this context, Jesus' cry of lament over mothers becomes one of His darkest sayings. Indeed: "Woe to those who are pregnant and to those who are nursing babies in those days!"

Flee to the Mountains:

Jesus' warning to flee to the mountains in verses 16-18 is an important part of His warning, too. Jesus was warning them to flee because, according to Josephus, once the Roman army began their attack they smothered the city to death. Once it began there was no escape. They starved the city by cutting off trading routes, making food sparse. Jesus' warning here was to flee before that entrapment began.

One will be Left:

One of the most misunderstood predictions in this passage is about the one who is left and the other who is taken. This comes from Matthew 24:37-40 and the parallel passage of Luke 17:26-36. Rapture theorists will often try to say that Jesus is describing the rapture here, but this is yet another prime example of their failure to take context seriously.

It may appear in this text that the rapture is taking place when one is taken and another is left, but Jesus is using clear Old Testament story in these texts. This imagery has been ignored by rapture theorists entirely. But if you pay attention to the context in which Jesus is speaking, it's apparent that those who are "taken" are the *wicked* while those who are "left" are the *good*. Carefully examine Luke 17:26-36 and Matthew 24:37-40. You'll see that in these passages, those who are taken and those who are left are compared with Noah and the flood. During the time of Noah the flood took the wicked away, and not the good. This is the very clear analogy. These verses cannot be proof for the rapture, since the rapture claims that Jesus will take the good away and leave the wicked. Whereas this verse, in the context of Noah and the flood, says the opposite. It is a blatant and embarrassing error of rapture theorists to take this text and use it to prove the rapture because it plainly is a reference to the days of Noah. But this shows the cherry-picking tendency rapture theorists have when trying to prove their theory.

Earthquakes and Disasters:

Another parallel between Jesus' prediction and the historical account of what took place is the occurrence of various earthquakes and nature disasters. Josephus gives an account of these nature disasters, and of how terrible they were. Jesus called these the signs of the coming tribulation (Matt. 24:7,

8). These natural occurrences were of such significance that Josephus felt to include them in his account. If they were just minor details he would not have made note of them. But they were unmistakable, and therefore Jesus used these as signs for the Jews to know when it was time to flee.

There are several other examples that we could examine which reveal that Jesus directly foretold the events of 70 AD. But these few examples are more than enough to show that Matthew 24 has been misused by rapture theorists to prove their doom and gloom philosophy. To rightly understand Matthew 24 is to see its parallel with the event of AD 70.

Instead of now listing every parallel, I want to continue by answering a few issues with the text that may have already arisen in your mind. Though, if you're interested, I do recommend a study of Josephus' account to see more parallels between 70 AD and Matthew 24.

Future Predictions in Matthew 24

The majority of this text in Matthew 24 foretells the destruction of the temple in 70 AD. However, roughly beginning in verses 29-30, Jesus begins speaking about His *future* coming. This is shown especially in verse 36. "But of that day and hour no one knows, not even the angels of heaven, nor the Son, but the Father alone." That Jesus is speaking of two different events, one which has already taken place, and another which is to come, has caused many to misunderstand this difficult chapter. But here I want to briefly show that the first half of the passage is a direct prophecy to the war of 70 AD, while the second half is a prophecy to the Christ's final coming.

If you look back to the beginning of this passage, the disciples had asked Jesus not one question, but three. They asked Him, "Tell us, [1] when will these things happen, and [2] what will be the sign of Your coming, and [3] of the end of the age?" (V. 3) They asked both about things happening soon, and things happening in the future. Jesus spends the rest of Matthew 24 answering their questions.

Verses 4-28 mostly give an account of what took place in AD 70. But with verses 29 and 30 (roughly), Jesus begins to describe that which is to come: His final coming and the consummation of all things. He switches focus with this statement. "But immediately after the tribulation of those days the sun will be darkened, and the moon will not give its light, and the stars will fall from the sky, and the powers of the heavens will be shaken." Here Jesus uses a well known, historically documented figure of speech. The astrological imagery of the sun, moon, heavens, and sky all mean the downfall of earthy empires and kingdoms. After describing the destruction of Jerusalem, He gives the disciples hope that one day the tables will turn. The kingdoms of this world will be subjected to the Kingdom of God. They will be overcome, and the Kingdom of God will reign eternally. This is also described at length in the book of Revelation. The statements of the moon and sun are not literal statements, but figures of speech well known to that era. With these statements Jesus is foretelling of the future day in which God will be "all in all" (1 Cor. 15:38). He tells of a day when all things will be made new, when the Kingdom of God will reign over all the earth, and consequently, when the kingdoms and rulers of this world will be subjected to His Lordship.

So it's helpful to see that Jesus was not merely telling of the destruction of Jerusalem in this passage, but also giving hope for the final resolve of all things when He comes again.

While there is much more that could be said to this regard, for the moment I feel it's unnecessary to go through the rest of Matthew 24 and try explaining what everything means. This is simply because that is not the purpose of this book, and also because several other brilliant individuals have given themselves to this task already. For more on this, see the recommended articles, videos, and books provided towards the end of this book.

Inconsistency

The interpretation of these verses according to rapture theorists is unfaithful to the text itself and especially to the historical context surrounding it. Their self-implied literalism is inconsistent in that they cannot take "in this generation" as an actual generation due to their preconceived conclusion. This inconsistency is yet another reason to doubt the rapture theorists assertion altogether. Matthew 24 is a prophetic passage with a partially-historical fulfillment, though rapture theorists have attempted to manipulate it into something else entirely.

8: A Second (and Third?) Coming

Quite simply, the rapture takes the second coming and implies a third. Saying that Jesus returns secretly first for those He raptures, and then another time for the final consummation of all things is wholly unfounded. And while not all rapture teachers place the rapture in this time period (often called a pre-tribulation rapture), they will still often break the coming of Christ into a secret second coming and a public third coming. However, there is no scriptural precedence for this. The bible makes it clear that Jesus *is* coming back again, but it will only be *once*. The rapture makes a claim otherwise, and this is yet another reason why it's a problematic belief we must leave behind!

My Framework: Partial-Preterism

Now, perhaps this would be as good a time as any to lay all my cards out on the table. Of the end times I believe in what is commonly called "partial-preterism". This means that I interpret the book of

Revelation, Matthew 24, Daniel 9, and several other scriptures as having been already fulfilled in 70 AD —though not in their entirety. Thus, *partial* preterism: partial (in part) preterism (in the past). I believe parts of these texts refer to our *past,* and parts refer to our future. I deduce this from the context and historical events surround the texts themselves. As it was shown in the last chapter, the historical accounts of 70 AD prove that many of these "apocalyptic" scriptures were fulfilled already in the first century. I make room for the bible to speak for itself, rather than what I impose upon it. Thus in studying this historical context, I've concluded that most of what today we considered our future is really our past.

This is the framework in which I work out my eschatology. At the moment I don't feel like it's necessary to argue any more on this point (any more than I already have), though I do hope to give you a simple summary of what I believe and what I'm leading you towards.

As a partial preterist, I still believe in the second coming, the resurrection, and the new creation of all things with the reign of God's Kingdom. The major difference, however, is that I believe many of the prophecies for destruction and calamity have already been fulfilled in 70 AD. This allows for an optimistic perspective of the end times. I truly believe that the world will only get *better*. Things may look bad from time to time but eyes of faith will see that God is still with us and has not forsaken us. He is active, present, and moving with us in history towards the final consummation of all things.

I recommend the book *Victorious Eschatology* by Harold Eberle and Martin Trench for a clear, biblical look into partial-preterism. You don't have to become a preterist to leave the rapture behind, but it's helpful to know this is my framework—a framework, I believe, of hope.

In Summary

This is what I believe:

Jesus is coming back for His bride. His Kingdom will reign on this earth. The dead will rise again to new life, in a brand new world. All things will be new. Jesus will justly judge the nations. He will have the final word, a word of life, a word of love. Death, the last enemy, will be destroyed. And we will live forever in the joy of the Father, the love of the Spirit, and the friendship of the Son.

But in the rapture, alongside the futurist predictions of doom and gloom, I do not believe. When examined against historical context, the book of Revelation and other apocalyptic accounts cannot be interpreted in a futurist way. In the context of this historical understanding, proven by the writings of Josephus, these texts refer to a past event: the destruction of the Temple.

In simple terms this summarizes my eschatology. I still hold to a classically "orthodox" understanding of the end times (which is the return, the resurrection, and the coming Kingdom), but I reject the modern invention of a futuristic interpretation. Instead, I hold simply to a "Theology of Hope" (as Jürgen Moltmann so aptly named it). Such a theology of hope is based on the resurrection of Jesus Christ as our hope, and as our expectation. The world is heading towards a resurrection like His, not towards destruction. Jesus' resurrection is the first fruit,[19] the pattern of our resurrection to come. The cross is behind us, metaphorically speaking. We now look forward to the resurrection of the dead. This

---

[19] 1 Cor. 15:20

"Theology of Hope" is my confession, my summation of belief.

> In the context of these expectations of life, His [Jesus'] resurrection must then be understood not as a mere return to life as such, but as a conquest of the deadliness of death—as a conquest of god-forsakenness, as a conquest of judgement and of the curse, as a beginning of the fulfillment of the promised life, and thus as a conquest of all that is dead in death, as a negation of the negative (Hegel), as a negation of the negation of God.
>
> It is then understandable, further, that Jesus' resurrection was not seen as a private Easter for His private Good Friday, but as the beginning and source of the abolition of the universal Good Friday, of that god-forsakenness of the world which comes to light in the deadliness of the death of the cross. Hence the resurrection of Christ was not understood merely as the first instance of a general resurrection of the dead and as a beginning of the revelation of the divinity of

God in the nonexistent, but also as the source of the risen life of all believers and as a confirmation of the promise which will be fulfilled in all and will show itself in the very dealings of death to be irresistible. [20]

---

[20] Jürgen Moltmann, *Theology of Hope* P. 211

9: Perverting Jesus

Jesus Christ is the "visible image of the invisible God." (Col. 1:15) When we look to Jesus we look straight into the heart of who God is, the revelation of His nature and being. All that we say about God must be held accountable to Jesus Christ. If we imagine that God is anything other than what's been revealed in His Son, we are fashioning an idol. God is like Jesus, and Jesus is like God.

And so, if God is like Jesus, God wins by losing, overcomes death by dying, and heals pain by suffering. Jesus is at once the innocent, slaughtered lamb of God, and the triumphant, roaring lion of Judah. Jesus reveals that God is sovereign over all the earth. But also that *this* God became a helpless child crying alone in a manger.

Any theology that emphasizes one aspect of who God is over another will promote a distorted vision. When we think about God it's important to keep both images in mind. God truly is the slaughtered lamb who has overcome. *This* is how God has revealed Himself. Yet Jesus, the suffering servant, is also a triumphant lion. He is a lion who acts like a lamb, and a lamb who is victorious as a lion.

The problem with the rapture is just that. It emphasizes the lion to come over the lamb who was, making the Jesus of the gospels somehow *different* from the Jesus who is to come. Rapture teachers will slyly say things like, "God came as a helpless lamb but He will one day return as a fierce lion!" It's almost as if they're trying to say that Jesus, once known for grace and mercy, will come again filled with an angry, wild blood-lust, killing the very humanity He died to save.

This inconsistency is dangerous. If Jesus did not truly reveal what God is like, then the whole fabric of the gospel is in danger of being undone. The gospel is not just the news of Jesus Christ, it is also the news of the Father of Jesus Christ. It is the message of God's good-pleasure towards humanity. It is a revelation of the Blessed Trinity, and our invitation to join their fellowship. God has become a man because He is that deeply interested in us. He wills the best for us. He came to adopt us as His sons and daughters.

But when the rapture happens, many of its proponents say that those left behind will suffer His furious anger. As if Jesus will return without grace or mercy. Yet how is that possible? Will God change His mind about humanity? Will He change His "yes" of affirmation uttered in Jesus Christ to a "no" of damnation? Will the Jesus who comes again really be anything other than the Jesus who suffered and died?

The revelation of who God is, that God is good and for the human race, cannot be undone by eschatology. Christology cannot be inconsistent with eschatology (our understanding of Jesus with our understanding of the end times). The Christ who was is the same Christ who is to come. If this is true then the same Jesus who extended grace to sinners and tax collectors, healed the broken and hurting, and preached the good news of God's favor will be the Jesus who comes again.

It's unacceptable for rapture theorists to subtly create a second Jesus to fit into their ideology of a pessimistic end times. Will the Blessed Trinity give up on humanity so quickly? If we truly believe that Jesus is what God is like and God is like Jesus, we absolutely cannot believe that God will abandon humanity—even and especially in the end times. Because that is simply *not what God is like.*

Hearing and Seeing

In Revelation 5 John writes a clever word picture to combat this belief. He writes about *hearing* the pronouncement of the lion, while *seeing* the lamb. With this John shows that God is like a lion who looks like a lamb. He is the triumphant savior, the victorious King. But He looks and acts like an innocent lamb. This speaks volumes about how God deals with problems. He is not a vicious lion who forces His will on mankind. He is the lamb who wins us over through suffering and weakness.

How does God overcome sin? He dies. He suffers. He is strong by becoming weak, He overcomes by becoming the victim of our corruption. This reveals so much about the God we believe in. With this passage John tells of a word-picture to describe it. Jesus is the slain lamb. We look at His suffering and we see that *this* is what God is like. But we hear that His suffering has turned into victory. He is the King. He is the lion who has overcome the grave.

It's important to always keep our eyes on the lamb who was slain while hearing of the lion who is triumphant. God is the suffering lamb, victorious as a lion. This is true for all times, even the end of times.[21]

This picture is quickly forgotten by rapture theorists who are eager to proclaim Jesus the violent man instead of Jesus the suffering servant. They are quick to show the lion and whisper the lamb, but scriptures show we must speak the lion and show the lamb.

In the end it will not be Jesus the Zeus-like-God that comes again. It will be none other than Jesus the crucified and risen savior. The god of the rapture is a myth.

The God of the Rapture

The god of the rapture is a schizophrenic god, a god of disproportion, a god who has gone back on His word in Jesus Christ. The god of the rapture is the god who *wills* chaos, destruction, and death. He is a

---

[21] See further N.T. Wright's comments on this passage in *Revelation for Everyone.* See also the works of Jürgen Moltmann, who has been on the forefront of re-understanding God in the light of the crucifixion as the crucified One.

god who "steals, kills, and destroys"—a role the devil and the devil alone is said to play.[22]

The rapture has made god into a devil.

The god of the rapture is angry, judgmental, and short-tempered. He's not a good father. He's a drunken, out of control father beating his children and spitting curses at them. Far from the God of Jesus Christ, the god of the rapture is a god opposed to sinners (instead of the God who eats with sinners, who is their friend). This god hates this earth. This god hates mankind—unless! they perform this or that or some other religious list of graceless requirements. This god is the god who says, "Love me—or else!" This god is a manipulative god worse than all the evil step-mothers, or wicked witches dreamed up in fairytales. A god with limited mercy, but quick to punish, quick to lash out in wild rage—this is the god of the rapture.

This is the theological legacy of the rapture. This vision of god is one of the most repulsive, disturbing inventions in all Christianity. I would count it amongst some of the worst heresies the church has ever faced. But we are no longer denying the divinity of Christ or the Trinity anymore. The new heresy is

---

[22] John 10:10

to deny that God is good. This is the challenge Christianity must overcome. As theologian, I am passionate about seeing such a god dismantled and removed. It is not a god at all. It is a myth. The god of the rapture spits in the face of Jesus Christ. I hope to reclaim the vision of God as absolutely, inexhaustibly, undoubtably good.

It is the kindness of God that leads men and women to repentance! (Rom. 2:4) It is not this nightmarish image of an angry deity that saves. It is kindness, goodness, and a vision of the God revealed in Jesus Christ, the God of love, of mercy, of justice.

Let's leave the rapture behind. Let's leave the *God* of the rapture behind. Let's go back to Jesus. Let's go back to the lamb of God who defeated the darkness of our world with humility, with death, and who wins our hearts through kindness. Let's return to the God is who *good.*

10: Perverting Jesus' Mission

The most well known prayer in the scriptures has to be the Lord's Prayer: "Our Father who is in heaven, hallowed be Your name. Your kingdom come. Your will be done, on earth as it is in heaven. Give us this day our daily bread. And forgive us our debts, as we also have forgiven our debtors. And do not lead us into temptation, but deliver us from evil. For Yours is the kingdom and the power and the glory forever. Amen."

Have you ever noticed just how much The Lord's Prayer is about *this* world? It's not a prayer of transcendental, mysticism. It is a very practical prayer: God, keep us fed. God, forgive us and give us grace to forgive others. God, may earth look like heaven. God, may your will be done here.

It's not a prayer of spiritually abstract hoopla. It is concrete and practical. It is earthly.

Jesus' mission might also be summarized with this prayer. He came to preach the Kingdom, advancing God's will on this earth. He came to heal, forgive, and set free. He came to redeem this place we call home. He built something here on earth that continues to this day. And it will continue on until He returns to consummate all created things.

But if the rapture is true, I think Jesus' prayer would have been a lot different. In fact, the rapture seems to take this prayer and flip it completely upside down. The rapture prays: "Lord, may we leave this earth behind and join you in heaven. May your will be done in heaven as in heaven where we want to be. Your Kingdom is there and we want to go there, please come take us there soon. Amen."

The rapture works against the mission of Jesus. God sent Jesus to advance the Kingdom here, to make earth look like heaven. But the rapture attempts to undo this mission when it expects the earth to look like hell, and for us to escape into some spiritualized idea of a heaven.

But God never planned to do away with the earth. He plans to recreate it, and to make it His dwelling place. Revelation 21-22 shows this in a beautiful vision of what's to come. Heaven and earth will be made one. God will dwell with us, His people. All will be made gloriously new. Justice will triumph, mercy will reign supreme, and love will become the atmosphere we live in.

The rapture has it backwards. If Jesus' mission is for the Kingdom to be established here on the earth, then why would we escape it? Why are we so obsessed with leaving this world behind when God has called us to make earth look like heaven?

The rapture cannot be true because it goes against the very fabric of Jesus' mission on earth. Instead of taking us away from this place, Jesus came to invade our world with His. He came to bring heaven to earth. But we have been trying to escape earth for heaven! We must learn to pray again with Jesus, knowing that we are not escaping this world but ushering in the eternal reign of the Kingdom of God.

We have a job to do here on this earth. We cannot become short-minded or quick to abandon it!

The day will come when all things will be made new. This means nothing will be lost or forgotten in the end—including and especially this beautiful earth.

It is a part of Christian belief in the resurrection to assert that nothing is ultimately unwanted, nothing finally lost or forgotten. When the last trump sounds and the sea gives up its dead, whatever was neglected or cast aside will be raised up and kept forever in the presence of the one in whom Memory and Love are joined.[23]

---

[23] Benjamin Myers, *Salvation in My Pocket*

Afterword: What Now?

The rapture has given purpose to the lives of many individuals. Without it, their place in this world just doesn't seem to exist. If we are no longer heading towards a rapture, but are on this earth for the long-haul, the question arrises: what are we to do here? If we're truly on this earth for good, what in the world are we to do now?

Belief in the rapture is a blinder over the eyes of those who believe it. Once removed we're able to see God's plan for the human race and the earth. In a way, for years the rapture has given fuel to a mindset which says, "to hell with the world, I'm going to heaven soon!" This short-sighted (and honestly very selfish) mindset lies under the surface of many rapture theorists beliefs, whether they'd admit it or not. But I hope I have been able to show that such a way of thinking is unscriptural and inaccurate. We are not leaving this earth anytime soon. We're here to stay, and we have a job to do while we're at it.

So then what *is* God's plan for the cosmos? If a "mindset of escape" is no longer an option, then what are we to do?

In simple terms, I believe our purpose here could be summed up in a single word, one used quite often in the apocalyptic literature of the bible: *justice.*

Justice means making right that which is wrong. So simply ask yourself: what's wrong with this world?

And there you have it. That is God's will for the cosmos. What came into your head right now? Was it poverty, hunger, social injustice, sex slavery, the environment, government corruption, war, or any number of the many injustices in our world?

You partnering with God to bring justice here is His will. Because this is leading to the renewal of all things, the time in which God will come and dwell with us here.

It really is that simple. Go find what drives you crazy about the world and ask God to help you fix it. Then get up and actually go do something about it. When we stop sitting around staring at the clouds waiting for our rescue and start doing something about making justice reign on the earth we will help usher in the Kingdom of God here and now. Imagine if all that energy we've devoted to fixating on the rapture went towards helping make the world a better place? What if all the money we as a church spend every year on the latest books by the newest doomsday prophets about the end of the world was spent instead on eradicating poverty, or ending world hunger? We're here for the long-haul whether we like it or not so we better start making this place look a little more like home. God will give us the strength, the courage, and the tools. We just need to see that this world is waiting for us to get our heads out of the clouds and partner with God to make earth look like heaven.

That's justice: when heaven comes to earth, and God's will is done through our lives.

That's the purpose of this book. It is a plea to the church of Jesus Christ all around the world: let's leave the rapture behind for good, and in exchange let's pick up a burning passion for God's justice on this earth.

I've tried to prove as exhaustively as I can the fact that the rapture is wholly unbiblical, unhistorical, and, frankly, dangerous. I know not everyone will agree with me or be convinced, but I hope at least to have opened up some eyes and ears to see the truth.

Because we need you here on this earth. We need people who are fully present and active in making this world a better place.

In the spirit of hope, I'll leave you with one of my favorite quotes from Martin Luther:

"Even if I knew that tomorrow the world would go to pieces, I would still plant my apple tree."

Recommended

In this short book it is nearly impossible to provide an answer to every question that arrises. However, I recommend the following articles, videos, and books by respected scholars and theologians to help in answering what I have left unanswered. These sources also serve as a great place to start for further study into eschatology as a whole.

Articles/videos:

"Farewell to the Rapture" by N.T. Wright - http://ntwrightpage.com/Wright_BR_Farewell_Rapture.htm

  - A short essay on the rapture by one of the world's leading theologians.

"On the Rapture" by N. T. Wright - https://www.youtube.com/watch?v=Kxzf00grErw

  - A short interview where this renowned theologian describes why the rapture is unbiblical.

"Lecture on Death, Resurrection, and the Afterlife" by N. T. Wright - https://www.youtube.com/watch?v=HXAc_x_egk4

- A lecture which gives an excellent overview for re-understanding heaven, the afterlife, and the end times.

"The End of the World as You Know It" by Greg Boyd - https://www.youtube.com/watch?v=HoWHzuYF798

- A series of teachings done on the book of Revelation and the end times.

"Rapture: Prophecy or Heresy?" by H. Speed Wilson - http://www.preteristarchive.com/dEmEnTiA/1989_wilson_rapture-heresy.html

- Several great textual analysis of common scriptures used in support of the rapture theory.

"The Destruction of Jerusalem" by George Peter Holford - http://www.bible.ca/pre-destruction70AD-george-holford-1805AD.htm

- A modern account of what took place in AD 70.

"The Rapture: a Popular by False Doctrine" by Cecil Maranville - http://www.ucg.org/world-news-and-prophecy/the-rapture-a-popular-but-false-doctrine

- A short, concise and accurate analysis of 1 Thessalonians 4

Books:

Victorious Eschatology by Harold R. Eberle and Martin Trench

- Teaches partial preterism. Read to understand in detail Matthew 24, Revelation, Daniel 9, and other passages.

Surprised by Hope by N. T. Wright

- An important work to reframe our understanding of heaven and the afterlife.

Revelation for Everyone by N. T. Wright

- Simple analysis of the book of Revelation.

In the End—the Beginning by Jürgen Moltmann

The Trinity and the Kingdom by Jürgen Moltmann

- Really any book by Jürgen Moltmann is worth your time. But especially this one in terms of understanding God as the "lion and the lamb", as the God who suffers with mankind in order to overcome suffering. See also *The Crucified God* and *Jesus Christ for Today's World.*

Raptureless by Jonathan Welton
   - A simple, and thoughtful introduction to why the rapture is a problematic belief.

The Improving State of the World by Indur Goklany (2007)
   - Statistics about our ever improving world.

The Jewish War by Josephus
   - You can usually find this text for free online somewhere. This book gives an account of what took place in 70 AD.

ABOUT THE AUTHOR

Stephen D. Morrison is a young, creative author and theologian passionate about recapturing the gospel of Jesus Christ as truly *good* news. He writes with a fresh perspective of the Christian faith by bringing together the traditions of the early church, and the insights of modern theology. He writes in a theologically challenging, yet clear manner, hoping to reach not only the scholarly but also the everyday person.

The major influences to his theology include Karl Barth, T. F. Torrance, and Jürgen Moltmann, alongside the early church fathers St. Athanasius, and St. Irenaeus.

Stephen is joyfully married to the love of his life, Ketlin. He graduated from Bethel's School of Supernatural Ministry in 2013, and as since retained a passion for God and for understanding Him theologically. He enjoys reading, traveling, and spending time with his wife.

Stephen currently lives in between places, jumping across the Atlantic a few times each year between Tallinn, Estonia and the United States.

Stephen is the author of *We Belong: Trinitarian Good News* and *Where Was God?* For more about Stephen please visit his website www.SDMorrison.org. Be encouraged to connect with Stephen on Facebook (https://www.facebook.com/StephenMorrisonMinistryPage/), and Twitter (https://twitter.com/morrisonsdm).

More from S. D. Morrison:

WE BELONG

Trinitarian Good News
By S. D. Morrison

We Belong: Trinitarian Good News seeks to answer two important questions: first, what is the gospel? and second, why is the gospel "good news"? With help from some of the greatest theologians in Christendom, S. D. Morrison seeks to beautifully and simply write about what should be the most important topic for a Christian: the gospel. Join him in re-discovering the amazing message of Jesus Christ, the breathtaking truth about who God is, and the hope we have in Him. Both theologically challenging and practically applicable, this book aims to be at once highly informative and life changing.

We Belong has been called "incredibly relatable" and "an insightful book written by someone [who] has been asking great questions."

Available now through Amazon: http://amzn.to/ 1UKopVA

WHERE WAS GOD?

Understanding the Holocaust in the Light of God's Suffering

By S. D. Morrison

In *Where Was God?* theologian S. D. Morrison presents the three most common responses to the Holocaust event (determinism, atheism, and unknowing) along with a fourth option which seeks to be "truly theological". Written as a conversation between friends, this book is easy to read while presenting deep and important conclusions. The Holocaust event is one of this century's greatest dilemmas. This book strives to give a clear, Christian response to its happening. Where was God? Does God remain indifferent to human suffering? How can one remain a believer in the aftermath of such tragedies? All these questions and more are discussed in this short book.

Where Was God? has been called a "theological masterpiece", and "a thoughtful, conversational, delightful little book on a very relevant topic."

Available now through Amazon: http://amzn.to/1n03Ba6

Quotes for a Hopeful Future

The following quotes are collected from various authors to help cultivate a hopeful outlook towards the future, and to understand the resurrection to come and the new creation of all things.

On hope:

Ascetic Christianity called the world evil and left it. Humanity is waiting for a revolutionary Christianity which will call the world evil and change it.

    - Walter Rauschenbusch

Christianity is wholly and entirely confident hope, a stretching out to what is ahead, and a readiness for a fresh start. Future is not just something or other to do with Christianity. It is the essential element of the faith which is specifically Christian: the keynote of all its hymns, the dawn colouring of the new day in which everything is bathed. For faith is Christian faith when it is Easter faith. Faith means living in the presence of the risen Christ, and stretching out to the coming kingdom of God.

    - Jürgen Moltmann

America can't be doom, I'm living here.
   - Kris Vallotton

To think that things are going to get worse and
worse in the last days takes no faith.
   - Bill Johnson

Christians will never find that they are called to
anything other than hope—for themselves and the
world.
   …They live in and with and by the promise. They
seize it. They apprehend it. They conform themselves
to it. And therefore in their present life they live as
those who belong to the future.
   - Karl Barth

What we need, whether we are children, adolescents,
adults or the old, is a balance between experience of
the present and expectation of the future, between
the fulfilled moment and the beginning of a new day.
   - Jürgen Moltmann

Every form of worship will be destroyed except the
religion of Christ, which will alone prevail. And

indeed it will one day triumph, as its principles take possession of the minds of men more and more every day.

- Origen

Eschatological Core Values:

1. I will not embrace an end-time worldview that re-empowers a disempowered devil.

2. I will not accept an eschatology that takes away my children's future, and creates mindsets that undermine the mentality of leaving a legacy.

3. I will not tolerate any theology that sabotages the clear command of Jesus to make disciples of all nations and the Lord's Prayer that earth would be like heaven.

4. I will not allow any interpretation of the scriptures that destroys hope for the nations and undermines our command to restore ruined cities.

5. I will not embrace an eschatology that changes the nature of a good God.

6. I refuse to embrace any mindset that celebrates bad news as a sign of the times and a necessary requirement for the return of Jesus.

7. I am opposed to any doctrinal position that pushes the promises of God into a time zone that

can't be obtained in my generation and therefore takes away any responsibility I have to believe God for them in my lifetime.

8. I don't believe that the last days are a time of judgement, nor do I believe God gave the church the right to call for wrath for sinful cities. There is a day of judgement in which GOD will judge man, not us.

- Kris Vallotton

On the resurrection:

To the soul belongs the body, so there can be no salvation for the soul without bodily resurrection. To the human being there belongs human community, so there can be no individual salvation without a new community. To the human community belongs the natural environment of the earth and its inhabitants, so there can be no salvation for human beings without the new creation of the earth and the redemption of the whole sighing and groaning creation. God the Creator remains faithful to his creation in its redemption too, and 'does not forsake the works of his hands'. He doesn't give anything up for lost, and destroys nothing he has made. That is why in the Bible the redemption is called 'new creation', and this embraces 'everything' (Rev. 21:5). Because many ideas of redemption that are hostile to creation and destructive of the world have crept into Christianity in the course of its history, this must be so much stressed, even if the images about 'the resurrection of the body' and 'the new earth' have become alien to scientific thinking in modern times.

- Jürgen Moltmann

So many Christians have read John's book expecting that the final scene will be a picture of 'heaven' that they fail completely to see the full glory of what he is saying. Plato was wrong. It isn't a matter –it wasn't ever a matter –of 'heaven' being the perfect world to which we shall (perhaps) go one day, and 'earth' being the shabby, second-rate temporary dwelling from which we shall be glad to depart for good. As we have seen throughout the book, 'earth' is a glorious part of God's glorious creation, and 'heaven', though God's own abode, is also the place where the 'sea' stands as a reminder of the power of evil, so much so that at one point there is 'war in heaven'. God's two-level world needs renewing in both its elements. But when that is done, we are left not with a new heaven only, but a new heaven and a new earth –and they are joined together completely and for ever.

- N. T. Wright

What God did in Jesus, coming to an unknowing world and an unwelcoming people, he is doing on a cosmic scale. He is coming to live, for ever, in our midst, a healing, comforting, celebrating presence. And the idea of 'incarnation', so long a key topic in our thinking about Jesus, is revealed as the key topic in our thinking about God's future for the world... That is why the closing scene in the Bible is not a vision of human beings going up to heaven, as in so much popular imagination, nor even of Jesus himself coming down to earth, but of the new Jerusalem itself coming down from heaven to earth.

- N. T. Wright

The image of the End-time 'fire' is an image of the consuming love of God. Everything which is, and has been, in contradiction to God will be burnt away, so that the person who is loved by God is saved, and everything which is, and has been, in accord with God in that person's life is preserved... Judgement does not have a merely negative sense but above all a positive one. That is, it will not only destroy but will above all save; it will not merely dissolve but will above all fulfill. It is the annihilating No to all the powers hostile to God, and is the dissolution of the world of evil; but it is the saving and fulfilling Yes of creation: "Behold, I make all things new!"

   - Jürgen Moltmann

What we have to expect of the coming kingdom of God on earth as it is in heaven is nothing less than the cosmic incarnation of God, in which divinity and humanity interpenetrate one another mutually as they do in the 'incarnation' of the eternal Word of God and in the 'outpouring of God's Spirit on all flesh'.

   - Jürgen Moltmann

On 70 AD:

All this occurred [Matt. 24] in this manner in the second year of the reign of Vespasian [A.D. 70], according to the predictions of our Lord and Saviour Jesus Christ.

   - Eusebius

[Revelation] is subversive literature, basically telling the Roman Empire that their days are numbered.

- Gordon Fee

[Matthew 24] was most punctually fulfilled: for after the temple was burned, Titus, the Roman general, ordered the very foundations of it to be dug up; after which the ground on which it stood was ploughed by Turnus Rufus... 'this generation of men living shall not pass till these things be done'—The expression implies that a great part of that generation would be passed away, but not the whole. Just so it was; for the city and temple were destroyed thirty-nine or forty years after.

- John Wesley

In this discourse [Matthew 24] Jesus predicts the destruction of the temple, the destruction of Jerusalem, and the dispersion of the Jews, all of which took place in A. D. 70. The uncanny accuracy of these predictions is embarrassing to higher critics...

- R. C. Sproul

It is clear to me, given the use of the same apocalyptic language in the Old Testament, that the primary application of Luke 21 is to events that happened in AD 70. I do not believe that it is responsible to use material in this passage today as 'signs of the times' in order to predict the end of the world. I would argue the same for the book of Revelation.

- Greg Boyd

Made in the USA
Middletown, DE
30 April 2016